EVERYTHING AFTER

EBONY K RICE

Published by Eagle Care Publishing House
San Antonio, Texas
eaglecarehome.com

Author: Ebony K. Rice

ISBN: 979-8-218-90464-7

Printed in the United States of America.

DEDICATION

This book is dedicated to my husband, Andre-Ello Vines. Thank you for choosing life with me and for being a steady foundation for our family. Because of your commitment, I am able to walk fully in who God has called me to be.

It is also dedicated to my children, my everything after every storm. May you always seek God first, pursue your dreams boldly, and remember that through Christ, all things are possible.

TABLE OF CONTENTS:

WHAT IS AFTER

After

After the heartbreak

After the heartache

After the death

After the pain

After the addiction

After the failure

After the loss

After the disappointment

After the change

After the storm

After Everything

There is Victory, calm still waters of renewed strength

There is beauty, born from the breaking

There is purpose, woven through every tear

That's everything after

INTRODUCTION

Life has a way of taking us through seasons we never expected, moments that test our strength, our patience, and our faith. We experience storms that shake us, losses that break us, and waiting seasons that stretch us. Yet through it all, God remains constant.

This book is about how you get through those seasons. What to do before a season. How to manage during the season. And, most importantly, the after.

This book is about finding peace after pain, purpose after loss, and hope after disappointment. It's a reminder that every ending holds the seed of a new beginning, and that God can turn even the hardest chapters of your life into something beautiful.

Each page is a reflection of faith, growth, and grace. This was written to remind you that no matter what you've been through, there is still everything after.

This is more than a book, it is a challenge. A challenge to change your way of thinking about the difficulties in life. Take your time as you read. Let each chapter speak to your heart. Take notes to use throughout your everyday life.Reflect, pray, and allow God to meet you right where you are.

CHAPTER ONE

BEFORE THE AFTER: THE STORM

"When it looked like the sun wouldn't shine anymore, God put a rainbow in the clouds." – Maya Angelou

There is something about storms that can make you feel small. The thunder shakes your peace, the wind tosses your plans, and the rain blurs your vision. You can not see what is ahead, and you can not turn back because you've already come too far. In those moments, life can feel just like storms; loud, uncertain, and unpredictable. For some people, a storm is just bad weather. For others, it is a season. A season will test your patience, your faith, your relationships, and your strength. Before the "after" arrives, there is always the "storm," the place where you question everything you thought you knew about life and, for some, even about God.

The Calm Before

When life is peaceful, it is easy to feel in control. You wake up with a plan, everything falls into place, and you think, "I've got this." But storms don't send invitations. They don't knock before entering your life. They show up unannounced, even in the middle of your highest moments, and they demand your attention.

For me, the calm before my storm looked like success and routine. I had plans, dreams, and expectations. Everything seemed stable, until it wasn't. When the storm came, it didn't just shake what was around me; it shook everything in me.

When the Storm Hits

People mean well when they say, "Everything will be okay." But, when you're standing in the middle of chaos, those words can feel hollow. Because deep down, you don't just want things to be okay, you want them to make sense.

I remember lying awake some nights, wondering how I got there. How could something that felt so right suddenly fall apart? I was angry, hurt, and confused. I didn't want to pray; I wanted answers.

Truth is, God doesn't calm the storm right away, He calms you first.

The storms I faced came in many forms; loss, heartbreak, disappointment, and the shattering of a plan I had built my faith around. Each moment taught me something: the same God who allows the storm is the same God who gives you the strength to stand in it.

I found purpose in pain. I used to think storms were punishments. Now I know they are preparations. Every drop of rain is watering something in you: patience, humility, resilience, and dependence on God.

It took time to understand that storms are not meant to destroy us; they are meant to develop us. When God removes something, it is never to leave you empty, it is to make room for what is next.

When I lost what I thought I could not live without, I learned that God's presence was the only thing I truly needed. When people walked away, I realized they were not meant to go where I was headed. When I was forced to start over, I discovered that God had been planning a new beginning all along.

Standing Still

Psalm 46:10 says, "Be still, and know that I am God."

Being still doesn't mean doing nothing. It means trusting that even in the storm, God is working behind the scenes.

So I learned to be still.

I cried.

I prayed.

I rested.

I listened.

I learned to sit in my pain until it taught me what I needed to know. There is power in surrender. There is healing in silence. And, there is peace in trusting God with what you can not control.

After the Rain

No storm lasts forever. The sky eventually clears, and if you look closely, you'll see the rainbow. That rainbow is more than a symbol of beauty, it is proof that you survived. It is evidence of God's promise that after suffering, there will be restoration.

My rainbow did not appear overnight. It came slowly, through small blessings, unexpected opportunities, and quiet reminders that God had not forgotten me. Each time I smiled again, laughed again, or dared to hope again, I realized I was already walking in my "after."

The Lesson

If you're in the middle of your storm, I want you to know this:

It is okay to not be okay.

It is okay to feel tired.

It is okay to cry.

Just don't stop believing.

When I look back on the storms I have survived, I often wonder where I would be if I had quit… if I had given up… or if I had chosen disobedience over faith.

Every storm shaped me (you), strengthened me (you), and prepared me (you) for the next season. As I grow older, I understand that no storm is wasted. Each storm carries a lesson meant to grow you. Those lessons become wisdom for the journey ahead, guidance for the next battle, and testimonies for those connected to you.

Every storm teaches, strengthens, and develops the person God is molding you to become.

The same God who brought the sun out before will bring it out again. Storms do not mean the end of your story; they mean something new is beginning.

So hold on through the thunder.

Rest when you need to.

Pray when you can.

Worship while you wait.

Because when the clouds finally part and the rainbow appears, you'll understand that everything; every tear, every trial, every test, was leading you to your everything after.

CHAPTER TWO
THE WEIGHT OF LOSS

"To everything there is a season.. a time to weep and a time to laugh, a time to mourn and a time to dance." - Ecclesiastes 3:1,4 (NIV)

Grief is a weight that cannot be seen, yet somehow it changes the way you carry everything. Loss has a way of changing a person quietly; the world keeps moving, but a part of you realizes life will never be or feel the same again.

I had to carry the weight of loss many times. The first time was when my father passed away in 2013. I was eighteen years old, only six months away from my high school graduation. Before I could fully understand that kind of grief, another loss came. Three years and four months later, in 2016, my sister passed away. Then one year and nine months after that, in 2018, my grandmother passed away.

By the age of twenty-three, I had lost my father, my sister, and my grandmother. I remember sitting in nursing class during the first week, writing the speech for my grandmother's funeral with tears in my eyes. I was grieving, but I was still showing up. I was hurting, but I was still moving forward. With tears in my eyes, still I rose.

When my sister passed away, she left behind three children, two boys and one girl. My mother and I cared for them together, and over time, they became my own. I became more than an aunt. They called me Mom. In the middle of my own grief, I was learning how to love, nurture, provide, and keep going for children who had also lost so much.

Then in 2020, my mother passed away from COVID. That was the heaviest weight of all. Losing her felt like losing the person who had helped me carry everything else. And, just when I thought I could not carry any more grief, life brought another storm.

In March 2023, I found out I was pregnant. For a moment, it felt like the sun was finally breaking through the clouds. After years of helping raise my niece and nephews, I thought I was finally about to become a mother in a new way. But in April 2023, I had surgery for an ectopic pregnancy. The baby was growing in my right tube, and the doctor had to surgically remove the pregnancy and tie the tube.

I was faced with the pain of losing what I considered my child while still grieving the loss of my mother. Just when the light began to appear, the clouds formed again, and another storm came rushing in.

In that season, I had to make a decision. I could sit in grief and allow the weight of loss bury me, or I could get up and live a life that honored the people I had loved and lost. I chose to rise. Not because it was easy, and not because the pain disappeared, but because God still had purpose for me on the other side of the loss. Each loss shook me to my core and challenged my faith in Christ. There were moments when I questioned everything. Moments when grief felt heavier than hope and pain felt louder than purpose. I often asked myself: How do I continue to persevere after so much loss? Where does strength come from when your heart feels exhausted? How do you continue to have faith after saying goodbye forever to so many people you love?

If I am being honest, I had not yet learned what it meant to fully lean on God. For so long, my mother had been my strength, the person I could count on, lean on, and run to when life became too heavy. I never truly knew what it felt like to stand without her. But when I lost her, I was brought to a place where God was no longer just someone I believed in; He became the One I had to depend on.

The strength I needed was not something I could create on my own. It came from surrendering the weight I was never meant to carry by myself. Somewhere between the tears, the funerals, the responsibilities, and the heartbreak, God met me in the middle of my weakness and became the strength that kept me standing.

What I survived taught me that true strength is not pretending to be unshaken; it is continuing to rise while trusting God to hold together the broken pieces within you.

And that is where I discovered the power of strength.

CHAPTER THREE

THE POWER OF STRENGTH DURING THE STORM

"He gives power to the weak and strength to the powerless."
– Isaiah 40:29 (NIV)

Strength is one of those words we hear often but rarely stop to truly understand. We're told to "stay strong," "be strong," or "keep it together," as if strength is simply the ability to keep standing when life hits hard. But real strength, spiritual strength, comes from a place much deeper than will power or pride. It is the quiet confidence that even when you feel weak, God is still holding you up.

What Strength Really Means

For a long time, I believed strength meant pretending not to hurt. It meant keeping a smile on my face even when my heart was breaking. I thought being strong was about never letting anyone see you cry, never admitting when you are tired, and never asking for help. That kind of strength is exhausting. It is survival, but is not healing.

I learned that real strength does not come from hiding pain; it comes from surrendering it. Strength comes from saying, "God, I can't do this without You." True strength is not found in how much you can carry on your shoulders, but in how quickly you place it back into God's hands. This strength takes wisdom. Wisdom to know your limitations, but believing with Christ all things are possible.

Strength in Weakness

There are moments in life when you will feel like everything is falling apart; your plans, your confidence, your peace. Where there is destruction happening, is often where your strength must be ignited. When you have tried everything and nothing works. When you have prayed the same prayer and still do not see the change. When you wake up feeling like you have nothing left to give, God whispers:

"My grace is sufficient for you, for My power is made perfect in weakness." (2 Corinthians 12:9)

Strength begins where self-reliance ends. It is the moment you realize that your survival was not by chance, it was by grace. Every time you thought you could not make it, but somehow did. That was God's strength carrying you through.

The Gift of God's Strength

When you ask God for strength, not only does He gives you energy to push through a task. He also renews your spirit. He aligns your perspective so you can see beyond what's happening in the storm and trust what He's doing behind the scenes. Some days, God's strength looks like peace when everything around you is chaotic. On days when your motivation fuel is running low, strength looks like determination and perseverance. Sometimes, it is simply the courage to get out of bed and face another day.

God's strength fills the spaces where our human ability runs out. It reminds us that we were never designed to carry the world alone. We were designed to walk with the One who already has.

Strength and Purpose

The storms of life are not random; they are purposeful. They are designed to strengthen what God placed inside you. Strength and purpose are intricately connected, for the strength to endure pain pushes you toward your purpose. Every time you choose faith over fear, you build your spiritual muscle. Gaining strength is a workout. Every time you forgive when you could have held a grudge, you grow in grace. Every time you rise after falling, you prove that God's power is alive within you.

Strength doesn't mean you will not cry; it means you will not quit. Strength is not the ability to not feel pain; it means you trust that the pain has a purpose.

Letting God Be Your Strength

There is a difference between asking God for strength and allowing Him to be your strength. When you pray, "Lord, give me strength," you are asking for help. But when you say, "Lord, You are my strength," you are declaring dependence. One asks for a gift; the other acknowledges a relationship. Much like, what a father is to a child.

When you allow God to be your strength, you stop striving to fix everything yourself. You stop chasing perfection and start resting in His presence. You stop trying to prove your worth and start walking in His grace. That is where transformation happens. Not when you finally feel strong, but when you finally stop pretending you are.

Resting in His Power

Even Jesus rested. He prayed. He withdrew. He leaned on His Father. If the Son of God Himself modeled dependence, why do we think we have to do life alone? Rest is not weakness, it is worship. It is saying, "God, I trust You enough to pause."

When you rest, you allow your body to heal, your mind to reset, and your spirit to realign. Strength without rest becomes pride, but strength that flows from God's presence becomes power.

The Lesson

Strength is not a feeling, it is a foundation. It's not about pretending to be okay; it is about knowing who holds you when you are not okay. Whatever you are facing right now, you are not too weak, too broken, or too far gone for God to strengthen you.

There are days when you feel tired, unmotivated, or simply weighed down by life. On those days, ask God to give you His strength. Not the temporary strength that comes from emotion, but the supernatural strength that comes from the Holy Spirit. Some mornings, when the bed feels too comfortable and your energy feels too low. You must pray for your strength and God will meet you in those quiet battles.

The quiet battles of procrastination we face every day open doors to laziness which leads to discouragement, heaviness, and even depression. It slowly steals motivation and clouds purpose. Pray daily for God to fill you with His power. His strength will help you stay disciplined, complete daily tasks, and pursue the goals He has placed inside your heart.

Remember, leaning on God's strength is not weakness, it is wisdom. It is recognizing that we cannot carry ourselves through every season. With Him, even in our weakest moments we can become victors.

The same hands that created the mountains can rebuild your confidence, restore your joy, and renew your hope. When you can not walk, He will carry you. When you can not see, He will guide you. When you can not speak, He will understand your tears. Because real strength doesn't come from standing tall, it first comes from kneeling.

CHAPTER FOUR

STAYING ON COURSE DURING THE STORM: SET GOALS, WRITE THE VISION

"Then the Lord replied: 'Write down the revelation and make it plain on tablets so that a herald may run with it.' — Habakkuk 2:2 (NIV)

God will give you the strength to accomplish the goals and vision He placed inside of you. Vision is a powerful thing. It is the seed of destiny that God plants within you long before it begins to grow. Every purpose, every dream, and every breakthrough starts with a vision. A glimpse of what God desires to do through you and for you. Vision only comes to life when you are willing to steward it, and one of the greatest ways we can steward vision is by writing it down.

The Power of Writing It Down

There is something sacred about putting words to what God has whispered into your heart. When you write it down, it becomes a tangible record of your faith and a reminder of your purpose. Habakkuk 2:2 reminds us that vision is meant to be written plainly. God didn't say, "Think about the vision," or "Hold it quietly in your heart." He said, write it down.

Writing your vision creates clarity. It gives direction. It becomes a map for where God is taking you. It allows you to measure progress even when you can not see results yet. Writing reminds you that even small steps are signs of progress.

When life becomes distracting or discouraging, you can return to what you have written and remember what God spoke to you. Scripture promises us this truth:

"But the Advocate, the Holy Spirit, whom the Father will send in My name, will teach you all things and will remind you of everything I have said to you." — John 14:26 (NIV)

When you write the vision, God will bring it back to your remembrance right when you need it most.

What Should You Write?

Some readers may be asking, "What do I write if I don't even know what I want yet?" Start with God. You do not have to have every detail figured out before you begin. When your heart is aligned with Him, He will begin to shape your desires and reveal what is worth pursuing. Psalm 37:4 says, "Take delight in the Lord, and He will give you the desires of your heart." This does not mean God gives us every random want; it means that as we delight in Him, He begins to place His desires within us. He teaches us what to yearn for, what to pray for, and what to build toward. If you feel confused or unsure, write what you are praying for. Write what keeps coming back to your heart. Write the burden you cannot ignore, the dream that will not leave, the people you feel called to serve, and the areas of your life where you need direction. As you write, invite God into the process. Ask Him to make the vision clear, to remove what is not from Him, and to strengthen what aligns with His purpose for your life.

Simple, Short-Term, and Long-Term Goals

A goal does not have to be grand, for it to cause a powerful movement. Some of the most meaningful goals are the simple, daily ones, the small steps that keep you consistent when motivation fades. Staying committed to daily goals keeps you connected to the vision and strengthens your relationship with God.

Simple goals are what you can do today. They build momentum. It could be as simple as making your bed, drinking water, praying before your day begins, or completing a task you have been avoiding. Daily procrastination can make simple goals feel overwhelming, but when you take them one step at a time, they become manageable.

Short-term goals are what you can accomplish within weeks or months. These might include starting or completing a project, completing a course, saving money, or strengthening your prayer life. Short-term goals become achievable when you approach them little by little. You can not eat an entire burger in one bite. The short-term goal is finishing the burger; your simple goal is taking one bite at a time. The goal is to strengthen your prayer life. Your simple goal is to pray every day.

Think of it this way: building your home brick by brick; trusting that every prayer laid, every act of consistency, every sacrifice made, and every lesson learned becomes part of a foundation that will stand strong through every season. True growth is never rushed; it is built patiently and purposefully, with God as the cornerstone.

Long-term goals are the bigger picture. The dreams that stretch your faith. Owning a business, publishing a book, becoming debt-free, or growing into the person God has called you to be. When you divide your goals into simple, short-term, and long-term, you give yourself room to grow without pressure. You learn to celebrate small victories while remaining focused on the bigger purpose.

Pray Over Your Vision

Goals are not only checklists, they are conversations with God. When you pray over your goals, you invite Heaven into your planning. You are coming into agreement, "God, let this align with Your will, not just my desires."

Sometimes we set goals based on what we think we need, but God sees the entire picture. Prayer becomes the foundation that keeps you from chasing what is temporary and directs you toward what is eternal.

Keeping Up With the Vision

Writing your goals is only the beginning. Transformation happens when you remain committed to them. Life can get pretty busy. Distractions start to feel normal. Doubt easily creeps its way through. When that happens, return to what you have written.

Read your vision out loud. Speak it as a declaration over your life. When discouragement tries to settle in, your written words will remind you of God's promises. Consistency builds character. Even slow progress is still progress.

Don't Compare Your Journey

Comparison is one of the greatest enemies of progress. When you focus on someone else's timeline, you begin to doubt your own. Remember, what God is doing in your life cannot be compared to what He is doing in someone else's.

You are on a divine schedule. Your goals, lessons, and breakthroughs will unfold exactly when they are meant to. Your vision doesn't need to look like anyone else's, it simply needs to look like obedience.

The Power of Obedience

Obedience is the posture of a heart that fully trusts God. It is not always comfortable, but it is always rewarding. When you choose to follow God's instructions, even when they do not make sense to you yet, you position yourself for blessings that only obedience can unlock. Obedience requires trust in faith.

"If you fully obey the Lord your God and carefully follow all His commands... the Lord your God will set you high above all the nations on earth." — Deuteronomy 28:1 (NIV)

Obedience is not about control; it is about alignment. It is saying, "God, I trust Your way more than my own." When we walk in obedience, we learn that waiting is not wasted and gratitude becomes the attitude that keeps our faith alive.

Gratitude While You Wait

Being thankful for where you are in life does not mean you have given up on where you are still going. Gratitude is fuel for progress. When you thank God in advance for what you have written, you activate faith. You begin to live as though it is already done, because in Heaven's eyes, it is.

He gave you the vision, so it must come to pass, not in your timing, but in His.

"For the vision is yet for an appointed time... though it linger, wait for it; it will certainly come and will not delay." — Habakkuk 2:3 (NIV)

Always be thankful, but never stop believing for more. You can be blessed and still hungry for growth.

The Lesson

God has already placed the vision inside of you. "Take delight in the Lord, and he will give you the desires of your heart." - Psalms 37:4 (NIV) Your responsibility is to write it, pray over it, and trust Him to bring it to life through your obedience. Even if that looks like you taking a step blindly in faith. You trust God to order your steps.

When the enemy whispers, "Give up," chose praise instead. Obedience will help build the foundation of the vision that will become a reality.

This journey taught me a powerful truth: when God gives you a vision, He equips you to carry it. You must be willing to walk by faith, not by sight. Vision requires movement. Purpose requires obedience. And destiny requires discipline.

Don't underestimate the power of what you have written. Your goals are the blueprint of your purpose. So take a pen, find a quiet place, and write the vision plainly. Keep it where you can see it. Speak it until you believe it. When you begin to watch it unfold, remember this: you did not just write the vision, you walked it out.

CHAPTER FIVE

MOTIVATION DURING THE STORM: YOUR WHAT & YOUR WHY

"Whatever you do, work at it with all your heart, as working for the Lord, not for human masters." — Colossians 3:23 (NIV)

Motivation is the heartbeat of progress. Motivation is the inner spark that keeps you moving when your body is tired, but something in you will not let you give up. It pushes you to rise after failure, to try again after disappointment, and to keep going when the outcome is still unseen.

A spark of motivation does not last forever. It must be fed. The spark needs fuel to make it a fire! It must be renewed daily through faith, discipline, and purpose.

Transform Your Motivation Into Determination

Motivation may start the journey, but determination and perseverance is what finishes the job. There will be days when you do not feel inspired, when life feels heavy, and when progress seems slow. On those days, determination must take over.

Transform your motivation into determination. Time waits for no one, and you do not want to wake up one day realizing that precious time has passed you by. Focus on today, do not worry about tomorrow. One day you will wake up and the present will be what was once only a thought of the future. Get it done today so the future version of you will be proud of the past version who pushed through.

Do not focus on others or what they are accomplishing. Be your own competition. Motivation gets you started, but determination keeps you consistent. The people who reach their purpose are not always the most talented; they are the ones who refused to quit.

Time and Focus

Time is one of the greatest gifts God has given us, and how you use it reflects what you truly value. We often say we "don't have time," but the truth is, we make time for what matters.

If you are still breathing, you still have time to accomplish the vision. Every minute you spend is a seed you are sowing; either toward your future or toward frustration. You must sow your seeds in the right direction.

Ask yourself daily: Is what I am doing right now helping me move closer towards my vision? If not, refocus and redirect your energy toward what matters most. Let every hour carry intention and every effort hold purpose.

Count Your Blessings

Gratitude is an essential fuel for motivation. It is easy to focus on what you do not have or what has not happened yet. When you pause and look around, you begin to realize how far God has already brought you.

Learn to count your blessings daily. Many of your everyday complaints are actually blessings when viewed from an optimistic perspective. The more you focus on what is right, the more strength you will have to fix what is wrong. Gratitude shifts your perspective from “Why me?” to “Thank You, Lord.”

A thankful heart does not deny challenges; it chooses to see the blessing already present within them. When you focus on what is still there instead of what is missing, you begin to recognize God’s hand in the details, the daily mercies, quiet victories, and answered prayers.

Who or What Are You Doing It For?

Every purpose needs a reason. This is your why.

Your why is the anchor that keeps you grounded when storms arise. It is the motivator that pushes you forward when quitting feels easier than continuing. Maybe your why is your family, your children, your faith, or the future version of yourself you are becoming.

Write down your why. Speak it out loud. Keep it in front of you when the journey gets hard. Because when your why is strong enough, your how will always find a way.

Your why must begin and end with God. He is the source of your strength, the guide for your steps, and the reason you refuse to give up. My in between includes my children, my husband, and my family; the ones who look to me for faith, hope, and example.

When you are determined to break generational curses and establish a legacy of blessings, healing, and restoration. God will work miracles through obedience. Not only in your life, but in the lives of everyone connected to you. Every prayer, every goal, and every act of faith plants seeds that will bloom for many generations.

Discipline: The Bridge Between Goals and Results

Motivation may help you start, but discipline ensures you finish. Discipline is obedience in action. It is choosing God's plan even when your feelings may resist it.

When emotions fade, discipline keeps you moving. Discipline keeps you working towards your goals even when no one is watching. Discipline keeps you faithful in the journey, even when progress feels invisible.

Discipline is not about perfection; it is about persistence. Consistency builds strength, and obedience brings alignment with God's purpose. Discipline shows God that you are serious about what you have been praying for. It is a daily declaration that you believe in the vision, even before you see it fulfilled.

Faith-Fueled Motivation

The greatest motivation comes from knowing you are not working alone. When your drive is rooted in faith, your effort becomes worship. Every step toward your purpose is a declaration that you trust God's timing.

Let your motivation come from obedience, not approval. You do not need validation from others when you are walking in your calling. As Eric Thomas says, *"Everybody wants to be a beast, until it's time to do what beasts do."*

Real faith requires real work. Purpose is not proven in comfort, but in consistency. Always remain consistent, even in turmoil. God blesses those who continue to show up trusting in Him.

The Lesson

Motivation may begin as a feeling, but it becomes a lifestyle when you commit to it daily. Each morning, you have a choice: to keep sleeping with your dreams or to wake up and chase them.

There are moments when I feel like quitting, when the vision feels heavy and the process is overwhelming. But whenever my strength begins to fade, I look back at where God has brought me from. Remembering His faithfulness reignites my drive.

My motivation does not come from ego or self-glory; it comes from obedience. I am simply doing what God has asked of me.

I carry this vision not as my identity, but as my assignment. I am walking out my purpose so my children will have the courage to walk out theirs. I want them to see faith in action, perseverance in motion, and obedience lived out daily.

Focus on your vision. Thank God for your blessings. Remember your why. Be intentional, disciplined, and faithful, because the same God who gave you the dream will give you the strength to complete it.

And when your future self looks back, you will smile knowing this:

You did not just hope for it, you worked for it.

You did not just talk about it, you became it.

CHAPTER SIX

THE WAIT: WHEN YOU WANT TO QUIT

"Let us not become weary in doing good, for at the proper time we will reap a harvest if we do not give up." – (Galatians 6:9 NIV)

There will come moments in life when you feel tired; not just physically, but emotionally and spiritually. You have prayed. You have worked. You have believed. Still, things do not seem to move as fast as you hoped or do not look like your vision. The temptation to quit will whisper to your heart: "Maybe this isn't for you. Maybe it's time to stop." Understand, just because you are weary does not mean you are done. You may be tired, but God is not finished yet. If your work does not look like the vision God gave you, good news God is still working. When you want to quit, that is often the very moment God is doing His deepest work.

Don't Get Weary in Well Doing

When you want to quit... don't get weary in well doing (Galatians 6:9 NIV).

It is easy to keep going when things are working out well. It is much harder when your effort feels unseen. Scripture reminds us that there is a harvest waiting, not for the fastest or the strongest, but for those who do not give up. You may not see the fruit of your labor right now, but that does not mean it is not growing. Some of God's greatest blessings develop in silence. You are planting seeds of faith with every act of obedience, and those seeds will produce a harvest in His timing. So do not stop sowing just because you have not seen the sprout. God is still working beneath the surface.

Pray, Rest, and Reboot

When exhaustion creeps in and your strength runs low, the answer is not to give up. You need to rest. While you rest, you must pray and wait. Psalms 46, verse 10 commands us to *"be still and know."*

Rest is not a sign of weakness; it is a strategy for endurance. It is an act of faith that says, "God, I trust You enough to pause." Pray, talk to God about what you are feeling. Tell Him about your frustrations, your fatigue, and your doubts. Then rest. Allow yourself to recharge, physically and spiritually. Take time to relax and reboot your energy.

Remember, consistency is key. The key to staying consistent is knowing when to run, when to walk, and when to rest. Even in stillness, you can be faithful. God values your pace as much as your persistence.

We must pour from our overflow. The Bible reminds us that we cannot pour from an empty cup, because we are the vessels God uses to pour out His love, wisdom, and grace. Before we can fill others, we must first allow God to fill us. *"Whoever believes in Me, as Scripture has said, rivers of living water will flow from within them" (John 7:38 NIV).* When we stay connected to the Source, we don't run dry. Our overflow becomes evidence of God's presence, refreshed, renewed, and ready to pour again.

Rest Is Temporary

Remember, resting is temporary. It is not quitting; it is repositioning. Rest gives you space to regain strength, refocus your vision, and reconnect with God. It is during rest that God renews your energy, restores your peace, and resets your focus on His plan rather than your own. Use rest as a time to realign. Sometimes God pauses your movement so He can adjust your direction. When you rest in Him, you trade exhaustion for endurance. This allows you to get into agreement with God, which places you in alignment.

Alignment with God's Purpose

Rest and prayer keeps you walking in God's steps, not racing ahead in your own plans. When you pause long enough to listen, God reveals what you may have missed while moving too fast. Alignment brings clarity. It strengthens your relationship with God and replaces anxiety with confidence.

Sometimes God delays what you want because He is developing who you need to be first. Some blessings can only be received once we become the renewed version of ourselves that God is calling us to be. Renewed in spirit, strengthened in mind, restored in body, and healed in heart. *"Do not conform to the pattern of this world, but be transformed by the renewing of your mind..." (Romans 12:2 NIV).*

The waiting season is not wasted time; it is preparation. When you trust in His timing, even your stillness becomes progress. Your waiting season is not empty, it is where your relationship with God deepens.

When the Wait Feels Long

Waiting seasons are some of the hardest. You may watch others move ahead, reach milestones, and live out prayers that look like the ones you have been praying for. Do not let comparison make you question your calling. Your timing is divine. What God has for you will not miss you.

Use the waiting season to strengthen your foundation:

- Pray without ceasing
- Rest without guilt
- Serve while you wait
- Keep your heart soft, your faith strong, and your eyes on God

The waiting is where trust is built. When the promise finally comes, you will be ready to sustain it.

Many blessings require sustainability. God does not just want to bless us; He wants us to be able to carry and sustain what He gives. That is why stewardship matters. Jesus teaches this in the parable of the talents. Two servants multiplied what they were given, but one buried his gift. The master replied, *"Well done, good and faithful servant... You have been faithful with a few things; I will put you in charge of many things" (Matthew 25:21 NIV).* He was pleased with the servant who was a good steward, the one who multiplied.

Sometimes God is waiting for you to become a better steward before releasing the blessing He has prepared for you. This is not to punish you, but to protect you. An unprepared blessing can become a burden. Waiting is not denial; it is development. God is shaping the discipline, wisdom, and maturity within you that is required to sustain the blessing that is coming.

The Lesson

When you want to quit, pray and wait. Do not move out of frustration, move out of faith. Every pause has purpose. Every rest builds resilience. Every delay deepens dependence on God. You are not behind; you are being prepared.

During waiting seasons, God often draws you into isolation, not for punishment, but for us to hear Him more clearly. Waiting becomes a sacred space where you can rest and replenish. In the quiet, I pray and wait for what is next, trusting God's timing while preparing for what's coming.

What you do in your waiting season, shapes the strength, depth, and intimacy of your relationship with God.

CHAPTER SEVEN

THE BIRTH OF AFTER: RELATIONSHIP OVER RELIGION

"Draw near to God, and He will draw near to you." – James 4:8 (NIV)

After every storm you have survived, every lesson you have learned, every moment you have waited, strengthened, or rebuilt, you will discover that the greatest gift of the entire journey is: God was not just developing your purpose. He was drawing you into a deeper relationship with Him.

There comes a point in every believer's journey when you realize that faith is not about routine; it is about relationship. Religion can introduce you to God, but relationship keeps you connected to Him. When you have a relationship with God, Christ, and the Holy Spirit, you begin to understand that religion is not mandatory. Religion is a guide, a structure designed to help draw you closer to God through worship and community.

Religion is like a vehicle that leads you toward God, but the fuel that keeps it moving is your relationship with Him. Without a relationship, religion becomes motionless like a car with no fuel. Religion without relationship is movement without direction.

Fueling Your Relationship

You must strengthen your relationship by fueling up often. Your spiritual "gas" does not come from ritual; it comes from intimacy with God.

How to fill your spiritual tank:

- Praying and talking to God daily: Talk with Him as you would a friend, not just when you need something, but when you genuinely want to be in His presence.
- Reading and studying Scripture to understand His heart, His promises, and His will.
- Listening to sermons or teachings that challenge your faith and encourage growth.
- Worshiping in song and spirit, allowing praise to become your prayer.

The closer you stay to God, the more clearly you will hear His instructions. When your relationship is strong, your faith will not only depend on Sunday service, it will sustain you every day of the week.

The Difference Between Religion and Relationship

Religion tells you what to do.

Relationship teaches you why you do it.

Religion focuses on rules.

Relationship focuses on love.

Religion can make you aware of God.

Relationship allows you to experience Him.

Religion is not bad; it serves a purpose. It is part of kingdom structure. Relationship is where transformation happens. It is where obedience flows naturally because love leads the way. When you truly know God, you stop serving Him out of obligation and start serving Him out of devotion. Devotion turns everyday living into worship.

Kingdom Business

As your relationship with God deepens, you begin to understand your kingdom purpose. Kingdom business is for those called to serve others for the fulfillment of God's Kingdom. Much like soldiers in the military, each trained and assigned a specific role.

If you're reading this, it's not by accident. You have a purposeful assignment to fulfill. Your gifts, your ideas, your compassion, they are tools God placed inside you to serve a greater mission. Your daily work, your willingness to help others, your acts of kindness that's kingdom business in motion. It's not just about what you do; it's about who you're doing it for.

Vessels on Assignment

We are vessels; living carriers of God's love, grace, and purpose. A vessel does not choose its assignment; it simply carries what the Creator pours into it. We are vessels on assignment, placed on borrowed time, entrusted with divine responsibility. Our assignment was chosen before we entered our mother's womb.

Every act of love, every word of encouragement, every seed of kindness are pieces of your mission. You are not merely existing; you are executing Heaven's plan on Earth. Because your time here is limited, you must stay filled. Stay connected to your Source. Stay prayerful. Stay willing. A vessel that remains connected to the well will never run dry.

The Lesson: Living in Relationship

Religion can help you find God.

Relationship helps you know Him.

Religion gives you a map.

Relationship gives you the journey.

Do not let routine replace connection. To live in relationship with God is to invite Him into every area of your life. Talk to Him in your car, while you cook, when you are working. Let Him be your daily companion, not just your Sunday appointment.

When you live with Him, peace follows you. Direction becomes clearer. You stop striving for outside approval and start resting in assurance. Relationship reminds us that God does not just want our service, He wants our heart.

CHAPTER EIGHT

AFTER EVERYTHING: THE POWER OF AGREEMENT

"Do two walk together unless they have agreed to do so?" — Amos 3:3 (NIV)

Amos 3:3 asks, "Can two walk together unless they agree?" The same principle applies to our walk with God. If we want to walk in His purpose, His peace, and His promises, we must first come into agreement with His truth. Agreement is not passive; it is a daily decision to align our thoughts, actions, and beliefs with what God says about us, even when our feelings, fears, or past experiences try to say something different.

Freedom is available, but it is not automatic. Many people pray for healing, purpose, peace, and transformation, yet continue living bound by fear, shame, insecurity, and the weight of their past. John 8:36 reminds us, "So if the Son sets you free, you will be free indeed." Freedom through Christ is already available, but walking in that freedom requires agreement. It requires choosing to believe what God says over what fear, pain, or past experiences try to declare over your life.

God will not force you to walk in freedom. He gives you access to it, but you must choose to step into it daily. You must renew your mind, challenge the thoughts that keep you trapped, and actively walk in the direction God is calling you toward.

As 2 Corinthians 10:4–5 reminds us, the weapons we fight with carry divine power to tear down strongholds. Many of those strongholds begin in the mind. The moment you stop agreeing with fear, shame, limitation, and defeat, and start agreeing with God's truth, your life begins to change.

When strongholds begin to break, your perspective begins to shift. And when your perspective changes, your mind is being renewed. Old thought patterns lose their power, and new truth begins to take root. That renewal changes how you see yourself, how you respond to life, and how you walk toward purpose. Ultimately, your outcome begins to change because your life is no longer aligned with fear, but with God's truth.

Freedom is available, but agreement is required. The moment you stop agreeing with fear and start agreeing with God's truth, transformation begins. As your mind is renewed and your faith is put into action, you begin to step into your everything after.

The Evidence of His Power

There was a time when I thought grief had taken too much, perhaps even everything from me. My father passed away six months before I graduated from high school, yet I still left for college as a first-generation student. During undergrad, I battled major depression, and many believed I should step away from school to focus on my mental health. Instead, I kept going. As I entered my final year of undergrad, my sister passed away. I began working nights to help care for her children while attending classes during the day, but I did not give up. I graduated and went on to nursing school. The week before classes began, my grandmother passed away, yet I continued and finished. While pursuing my master's degree, my aunt passed away, and only a few months after earning my degree, my mother passed away. At every major milestone, there seemed to be a storm waiting for me. Yet each milestone was connected to my purpose, and each storm taught me that giving up was never the answer. The trials were real, but so was God's grace, which carried me through them. He did not remove every storm, but He gave me the power to keep moving forward until I reached the other side.

His power did not always come in dramatic ways. More often, it revealed itself in the quiet moments when I thought I had nothing left to give. Sometimes it came as the strength to get out of bed. Sometimes it came as peace in the middle of a day I did not know how to face. Sometimes it came as provision when I could not see a way forward. And sometimes it came as purpose rising out of places I thought were only broken.

Looking back, I can see it clearly now. God was not absent in my grief. He was strengthening me, shaping me, and preparing me. What I thought would destroy me became part of the evidence of His power working in my life. He took loss and taught me compassion. He took pain and gave me purpose. He took what felt like an ending and began building my everything after.

That same power is available to you. His strength is not reserved for people who have it all together. His power is made perfect in weakness. When you surrender what you cannot carry, renew your mind with His truth, and keep walking by faith, you give God room to work through what you thought was wasted.

Do not just read these lessons. Live them. Pray through them. Write the vision. Do the work. Challenge the thoughts that keep you bound. Come into agreement with what God says about you, and allow His power to meet your obedience. Your everything after will not unfold because life was easy. It will unfold because God is able.

The Lesson

Living out these lessons is not about perfection; it is about progression. It is the daily decision to choose faith over fear, purpose over pain, and obedience over comfort.

As you continue walking forward, you will begin to see that nothing you experienced was wasted. Every storm strengthened you. Every setback taught you. Every season has prepared you for what comes next.

Your life is the evidence, and your walk is the testimony of your faith.

When you look back, do not focus on what you lost. Focus on what God built through it. Let your past remind you of His faithfulness, not your failures.

Everything after is not about becoming someone new. It is about fully stepping into who God has called you to be.

Do not let what you survived make you afraid of what God still wants to build through you. Keep moving forward with faith, trusting that the same God who carried you through every storm is still guiding you into everything after.

Walk boldly in the vision God placed inside you. Walk confidently in the purpose He prepared for you. And remember that if God is for you, who can be against you? (Romans 8:31)

This is your after.

Not the end of your story, but the beginning of everything God still wants to do through you.

The storm did not take you out.
The past did not define you.
The waiting did not stop you.

There will only ever be one you.

Run your race.
Finish your course.

The world is still waiting for what God placed inside of you.

Your everything after is waiting for you.

A PRAYER FOR THE READER

Heavenly Father,

Thank You for this reader, for their life, their story, and their purpose.

Thank You for guiding them through every storm, every season, and every waiting place.

Lord, remind them that You are in every detail, that no pain is wasted and no delay is empty when You are in it.

Strengthen their heart when they grow weary, renew their mind when they feel lost, and refill their spirit when it runs dry.

Help them to trust You in the waiting, to walk with You in the working, and to worship You in the winning.

Let their faith remain unshaken, their purpose remain clear, and their relationship with You be unbreakable.

May they continue to grow, to serve, and to shine, as a vessel carrying Your light wherever they go.

Let their "everything after" be filled with peace, purpose, and power, all for Your glory.

In Jesus' name,

Amen.

AUTHOR BIOGRAPHY

Ebony Rice is a faith-led author, visionary, healthcare professional, and founder of Eagle Care Homes. Her life is a testimony of perseverance, purpose, and the sustaining strength of God.

After walking through deep seasons of loss, including the passing of her father, mother, sister, and grandmother, Ebony learned what it means to rise through grief and continue pursuing purpose. Her journey also led her to help raise her niece and nephews as her own, shaping her heart for caregiving, family, and her Kingdom assignment.

Through her writing, Ebony encourages others to find strength in the storm, purpose in the process, and their "everything after" in Christ. Her message is rooted in faith, transparency, and the belief that God does not just give you a purpose, He prepares you for it.

www.ingramcontent.com/pod-product-compliance
Lightning Source LLC
LaVergne TN
LVHW090618110826
845146LV00001B/449

9798218904647